The Manageable Cold

THE MANAGEABLE COLD

POEMS

TIMOTHY McBRIDE

TriQuarterly Books
Northwestern University Press
Evanston, Illinois

TriQuarterly Books
Northwestern University Press
www.nupress.northwestern.edu

Printed in the United States of America

10 9 8 7 6 5 4 3 2 1

Library of Congress Cataloging-in-Publication Data
McBride, Timothy, 1956–
    The manageable cold : poems / Timothy McBride.
      p. cm.
    ISBN 978-0-8101-2675-6 (pbk. : alk. paper)
    I. Title.
  PS3613.C295M36 2010
  811.6—dc22

                                                              2010020993

♾ The paper used in this publication meets the minimum requirements of the
American National Standard for Information Sciences—Permanence of Paper for
Printed Library Materials, ANSI Z39.48-1992.

For Lee Sullivan, after all

This is the Hour of Lead—
Remembered, if outlived,
As Freezing persons, recollect the Snow—
First—Chill—then Stupor—then the letting go.

—EMILY DICKINSON

Contents

Acknowledgments   *xi*

ONE

Snow Fence   5
Rochester to Raleigh: December 1988   6
Bonsai   8
Grace After Meals   9
Small Change   10
Conn   11
Remnants   12
After the Rain   13
Vertical Hold   14
The Road to Oz   15
Squats   16
All Souls   17
Solar Plexus   18
Liston   19
Ecce Homo   21
Country Matters   22
Daily Round   24
On Hearing That Music Enhances Brain Development   25
Tyner   27
A Travelogue of Self and Soul   28

TWO

Young Girl with Flute   31
A Curiosity   33
If My Friend Should Tell Me   34
At the Park   35
In the Walls   36
Surgery Rotation   37
Slow Dissolve   38

Separation   39
Laundry Bag   40
Another Autumn   41
Atalanta   42
Our Sentence   43
Villainous   44

THREE

McMurdo Sound   47
An Urban Myth   48
At the Wolf Cage, Seneca Park, 1980   50
Ursa Minor   51
The Bird Feeder   52
Father Damien of Molokai   54
Horseman, Pass By: A Lunar Eclipse   56
Cave Canem   58
Man in the Moon   59
Those Are Pearls That Were His Eyes   60
To a Friend Whose Work Has Come to Nothing   62
By Blue Ontario's Shore   63
The First Sorrowful Mystery   64
Don't Use My Blood   65
The World's Fare   67
Powers   69
Self-Assessment in a Hotel Men's Room   71
Zale   72
The Afghan Buddhas   73
The White Doves of Mazar   74
Amontillado   75
Character as Fate: The Limits of Formulae   77

Acknowledgments

The author acknowledges and thanks the editors of the following journals, where versions of the following poems have appeared:

Journal of the American Medical Association (JAMA)
"Don't Use My Blood"
"Surgery Rotation"
"The White Doves of Mazar"

Shenandoah
"At the Wolf Cage, Seneca Park, 1980"
"Horseman, Pass By: A Lunar Eclipse"

Tar River Poetry
"The First Sorrowful Mystery"
"On Hearing That Music Enhances Brain Development"

Seneca Review
"Snow Fence"
"An Urban Myth"

Poetry Northwest
"Grace After Meals"

Nebraska Review
"To a Friend Whose Work Has Come to Nothing"

Greensboro Review
"Bonsai"

Cumberland Poetry Review
"Conn"

Plains Poetry Journal
"Rochester to Raleigh: December 1988"

Kentucky Poetry Review
"Squats"

Independent Weekly
"Liston"

The Manageable Cold

ONE

SNOW FENCE

What turned them against each other
was nothing they could say to me,
the grandson, who would come each week
to work for an hour or so
cutting the grass, raking leaves,
shoveling the sidewalk and the driveway.
It had all been settled long before,
agreed to, conceded: the separate rooms,
the silent meals, the reluctance even to speak
the other's name. ("If it's *him* you're after . . .")
"If it's *her* you want . . .") Something stark
and irreducible had come between them,
like the repeating decimals I'd seen at school,
the same failed answer piling up
over and over, grudging as the snow
that gathered each winter in the fence
it took the three of us to hang.
Clearer than any word or gesture,
I remember this, our one job together,
how they stayed each end of the coiled wire
while I moved back and forth along the ground,
stretching the frets to their angled shadows,
pounding the stakes at their feet. In a month,
a steep gray drift would rise
at the side of the drive
and curve between his windowsill and hers.
Each spring I'd rake around it,
the ice still trapped in the borders—
a remnant of our last and longest season:
split wood, storm shutters, the manageable cold.

"Canadian air," we called it. Those first
hard days it wrung all colors gray,
salted the sky to match our winter streets.
Some weeks you wouldn't know the sun was round.

Down here they're "Northern gusts." Tired, demystified,
they tow a spent but glowering snow-worked haze
that strafes dry leaves along the papered grass.
All winter long they sift what autumn sloughs,

threshing to music as the carolers,
unbooted, slush across my unraked lawn
through drifts of fist-sized maple, claws of oak,
wind-tattered hands that hush the fading songs

in raveled language redolent of smoke,
the vowelless rustling plaintive, distant, lost—
a counterpart in speech to daylong dusk
that tilts toward dark its dim refracted light.

This was our indoor sound, those Christmas dawns,
awash in what we'd ripped from wrapped-up gifts.
Our eyes gone pirate-wild in all that loot,
who cared what windings kept us locked in ice

or worried about culling gifts from chaff?
"Now ahhh . . . which is which?" our father laughed, then packed
the grate and held out tinsel straws:
The shortest one would get to throw the match

as soon as we had heard the chimneyed *whoooo.*
"Ghosts," he joked, "from Christmas past." "Melt them quick,"
the losers shrieked; our noses to the frozen glass,
we'd watch the sky rain down the large black flakes

and feel our thin partition weep and blear.
I always wondered why, when we turned back,
my mother's eyes looked stricken. "Let's have a song,"
she'd say, smiling now, leading us in,

still ten of us, again, another year.

BONSAI

With careful pruning and some copper wire,
our mother turned azalea shrubs to trees
in miniature, corkscrewing their trunks
and crooking their branches until they took
the crabbed and gnarled shape of rock-bound
olives she'd seen in photographs of Sicily
and Crete. She loved their ovate
fingernails of leaf, the way the jut wrist
of stump thickened at the base
to a flange of root break, moss, and weathered bark.

Ten months out of twelve, theirs was the stoic,
sculptured calm of Chartres's martyrs.
April made them something else:
One day they'd burst aloft in kites of bloom,
great parasols of pink and tangerine
thrown skyward in a wild and wondrous gasp,
as if the very scale and symmetry
she'd conjured from that potted inch of dirt
were but the fractions of this reckless yield.

GRACE AFTER MEALS

Our television old-hat black-and-white,
we gave the brand-new dishwasher a look.
Each night we knelt and hugged its warming hulls,
ears tight to the spun music, the peristaltic
churn and wash and hiss as wondrously strange
as what we'd heard beneath our pulled-up shirts.
What were stove and frigid air to this
dishwashing marvel, cattle-car portable,
gurneyed to the sink, its dual umbilicals
flexed to sterilize, contagion-free,
our Jericho of waste: a week-old pot
of mortared Rice-A-Roni, a fishbowl untenanted
through long neglect, even the *things adult*
we'd vaguely sounded out and named
adulteries—lipsticked gin and tonics,
cigar-muddied ashtrays, pewter and pilsner
smirched in sour beer—even these
streamed down the vulcanized spillway
past sight and sound and caring.
A squat, boxed promise, it glowed
green as dawn across its numbered dials,
no mistake beyond absolving, its staid
confessional calm guaranteed to reign forever,
whirled without end. "Amen," we answered,
cleaned and scrubbed and lullabied to sleep,
its broken iambs cradling our dreams:
Rinse-Wash-Rinse-Wash-Rinse-Rinse-Dry.

SMALL CHANGE

Father Conner gave us $2.50 a week
to stay after school for an hour
picking up wrappers and beer cans
around the playground and convent,
setting up chairs and tables for bingo,
mopping the cafeteria floor.
Parish priests are chiselers,
so one Monday when he asked,
"What if I pay you a penny today
and double it every day for a month?"
we looked ahead as far as Friday,
counted 31 cents, and said if it was okay
with him, we'd keep things the way they were.

We felt our error in his laughter,
and when he had gone,
we worked it out on the blackboard,
watching it widen day by day,
uneasy that the obvious had not been true,
strangely unconsoled by the refrain,
"He'd never've paid us anyway."

CONN

Light heavyweight champ Billy Conn had two fights
with heavyweight champ Joe Louis, narrowly losing
the first but being soundly beaten in the second.

Billy Conn once knocked my father out:
an uppercut in Pittsburgh, second round.
I've got the clipping. He was proud of it,
who'd lost at larger games with less renown.
"I stood five minutes with that fucking Mick—
and gave him hell." No win had meant as much.

He tried and tried some nights to make me see
how Conn had staggered Louis that first fight:
"He nailed him, Timmy, just like he nailed me,
a right hand, under." Then he'd have me do it.
Corner him. Beat him to the punch.
Lean in to learn what made his life go on:
five minutes' worth of hell with Billy Conn,
who took the crown from Louis. Almost. Once.

REMNANTS

Twenty years after he left South Orange,
our father still made *"are-inge"* juice
for breakfast. Though most of his words
had softened, his hometown spiked our drinks
and made us laugh: "What's in the pitcher?"
we'd ask, trying to trip him up. "What color
would you call this?" He'd frown and make us wait
("It's frozen concentrate." "I'd call it *brown*.")
until we squeezed it out of him, his past
reduced to pulp and pits in the mouths
of his children.
                        We helped ourselves to all of it.
When he spoke long-distance to his brothers,
we'd hang around the phone and imitate
their odd locutions (*breezeway, turnpike, harp*).
Whole afternoons, we'd trash the attic, looting
his letters and photographs. ("That's rich,"
some friend had written. "Who's this lady
in the bathing suit?" we'd ask.) How sure
we were that it all meant nothing to him now,
the old nicknames and girlfriends, the diary
he kept for half a year. How certain we were
it was all safely forgotten, stowed away
forever like the 45s we never heard him play.
The day we found the duffel bag
and pilot's wings he told us he had lost,
we showed up at his bus stop after work
decked out like flyboys. Arms wide as fighter planes,
we ducked beneath the slide rule he unsheathed
in mock distress as we attacked his legs
and dragged him to a slow, stiff-legged halt—
"Hey, Dad! We got you, Dad!"

AFTER THE RAIN

Our fathers hung their heads
and caught the bus, pounding
the pavement that was gouged
by plows and sown with salt
four months a year.
Each spring the blacktop
turned bone white and scuffed
our baseballs till they needed tape.
I knew each front porch
from my paper route,
knew which dogs barked
and which ones bit, fought
Lou Tallo in the vacant lot,
and kissed his sister
two weeks after that.
The postman had a limp
and hung his sweaty socks
on Brennans' hedges
while he ate his lunch.

Best were summer afternoons,
after the rain sent us in,
those rare days when the sun
came out again.
We'd race around the block
inside the steam, the clean
ozone scent a hint
of paradise,
as if from our cramped streets
something could rise.

VERTICAL HOLD

*Image stability has eliminated the "vertical hold"
dial on modern televisions.*

TV's deceptions were harder to miss
before they fixed this problem for good.

Before they fixed this problem for good,
the president's head would spin in circles.

The president's head would spin in circles,
like the roller towel in a public bathroom.

Like the roller towel in a public bathroom,
he stood for purity but wound up shit.

He stood for purity but wound up shit
(*"freedom . . . terror . . . terror . . . freedom"*)

(*"freedom . . . terror . . . terror . . . freedom"*)
loopy and blabbering, head in his ass.

Loopy and blabbering, head in his ass,
he couldn't really look us in the eye.

He couldn't really look us in the eye
because our resolution wasn't fixed.

Because our resolution wasn't fixed,
what we stared at sometimes made us sick.

What we stared at sometimes made us sick
and broke the hold that never now lets go.

THE ROAD TO OZ

But for the tornadoes and the leash law,
Kansas wasn't all that bad a place—
or so we're to find it at the last,
uncolorful, of course, no indulgences
for a girl's "Why then oh why can't I?"
but homey and forgivable in its boredom
after one has seen the wingéd apes,
the trees armed and ornery, one's own feet
pulsing out coordinates to a witch
with bad intentions. Never mind that the hag
on the bike will be back for your dog
or that the storm cellar was already locked
and bolted by the time you'd gotten home.
You've met the gold-brick Wizard and you've bowed
to the grinning useless Glinda of the North.
You know what lies beyond the rainbow now.

SQUATS

for Joe McCann and Jim Megna

Leg days hurt worst. At noon we'd alternate—
"Head up! Hips tight!"—honing the flesh to stone.
Nauseated, thighs thickened from the freight
that fueled the swelling gorge of blood and bone,
we'd goad each other, *"Get another rep!"*
and mock the iron's impaction of the spine.
Each week we'd up the load, another step
toward might and grace—Olympian design.

Such nonsense. Still, like me you're at it yet,
though grace and might seem less sublime than vain
and vanity not half what makes us sweat
not half what fuels compulsion in the brain:
that badger—born in anger, fed on pain—
sulks fat beyond this regimen of strain.

ALL SOULS

When I was twelve years old
I pressed a pumpkin seed
into a broken flowerpot
under my uncle's workbench
down in the half-lit basement
of his house on Genesee Street
on a rainy indoor day
and then forgot about it
until it rained again
and I was back downstairs
pitching a perfect game
against the cellar wall
with a beat-up tennis ball
that took a wicked hop
skipped past some car parts
smashed a quart of beer
and left wet bounce prints
leading me back down
under the workbench
to that broken flowerpot
unwatered and unwatched
exposing to me now
a six-inch bone-white stem
whose blind and beaded head
grown desperate for me
was monstering a dark
more black than Halloween.

I crushed it in my fist.
I lost my perfect game.

SOLAR PLEXUS

First times are confusing. When I was gored
to the earholes on Vince Cannella's helmet,
my numbered lungs unfastened: "This is it,"
I thought. "I've burst. I'm dying." My last word,
my involuntary Kurtzian *"hoarrrrrr,"*
bespoke the sudden hollow I perceived
in our devout teamwork, the dull familiar
thud of all for one. No, this crushed smother
this inconceivably monstrous knot of breath
was—*Eli, Eli . . . foul unknown softness*—mine.

Ah me. Two minutes later I was fine.
Chinstrapped, my mouthpiece set between my teeth,
I took the field the way a hooked gar
retakes the shallows: listing, suspicious,
aware somehow that none of this
prepared it for that moment up on shore.

LISTON

The year I learned to read,
his name was in the paper every day
like a leather rope on a gymnasium floor:
Lis-ton, Lis-ton, Lis-ton.

The night he decked Floyd Patterson,
they ran a life-sized photo of his fist—
a thick black cobblestone
15 inches in circumference.
"Man or Beast?" the caption asked.
At arm's length, his face was cropped
at the eyebrows, scowling,
out of focus.

His story was a tale-of-the-tape.
I knew it by heart: height, weight,
reach, chest (expanded/at rest).
I knew his record and his knockout rate.
Words I didn't know, I looked up:
baleful, illiterate, felon.

I learned that he was booed at every fight.
That "Negro leaders" prayed for him to lose.
That Marciano would have kicked his ass.
That he quit both times against Cassius Clay.
That no one knew the date of his birth.

In junior high, I read his obituary.
It said he'd been dead
between six and nine days

when they found him, slumped on the floor
in his own home. It said the TV was on.
That he was born in Forrest City, Arkansas.
That he was the 22nd heavyweight champion of the world.

ECCE HOMO

Former underboss Salvatore "Sammy G" Gingello used his influence
in Local 398 to squeeze our rival trucking firms. Gingello was
killed . . . by a remote-control car bomb.
        —*ROCHESTER DEMOCRAT AND CHRONICLE*

The night they blew up Sammy Gingello,
we walked down past the Eastman Theater
to the Blue Gardenia and pissed in his grave:
a three-by-four-foot pit in the pavement
at the corner of Gibbs and Stillson Streets.

It was after midnight. The cops had towed
the gutted limo, the crowd gone home,
and we were eager for a story to take
back to school, the chips of windshield glass
our proof of purchase: We were there.

So there we were, three long-haired altar boys,
eager to show how much we weren't afraid,
as though what these men killed for had no claim
on us: their envy, lust, and greed defused by
our blaspheming, *Baptizo te in nomine . . . diaboli,*

which we intoned with high solemnity
while drawing crosses on the open ground,
our unctions tinged with oil and gasoline
beneath a traffic light that gave us back
our mirrored faces red and gold and green.

COUNTRY MATTERS

The censors cut Ophelia's part from the Russian
film version of *Hamlet*.
        —AZAR NAFISI, *READING LOLITA IN TEHRAN*

Our teacher pointed out the "ugly pun"
in Hamlet's "country," but he never mouthed
the consummating "cunt." That too, too sullied/
solid/sallied flesh had to be tongued
trippingly into place—deformed, misspelled,
and well-encased inside another word
less leprous to the porches of our ears.
Blunt as stumps about Ophelia's rape
in Saxo's Latin *Danish History*
(she had it coming as a cunning whore),
the editors' semantic dispositions
turned timid at her Anglo-Saxon hips.
So "country matters" become "rustic doings,"[1]
"an indecency,"[2] "a pun on the pudendum,"[3]
until the puzzled student wants to shout,
"more matter with less art," since Hamlet
clearly thinks of little else—all Denmark's rot
putrefying and enseamed between
his mother's and his girlfriend's toothsome thighs.
Sharp stone incisors lock the castle gates
in Kozintsev's Russian film, a *vagina
dentum* nightmare that grips all Elsinore.
Within that bloody maw, Ophelia's "chaste
possession" is debased and "loosed" as bait
inside an iron corset. Such fatherly concern
was wasted on the censors in Iran,
who banned the film from Tehran's theaters
until Ophelia's part was cut.

(No Persian girl is fathered by a fool,
resents her brother's tips on chastity,
or goes insane when doing what she's told.)
In the Sahel, where no one's daughter ever drowns
or gets sent packing to a nunnery,
the parts they cut are real. A bare bodkin,
a tin lid, or a bit of broken glass
mutilates and scrapes away the clitoris,
promotes virginity, deadens all desire.
Sometimes the labia are sewn with thorns,
sometimes a struggling child will bleed to death—
frailty being another name for *woman*,
a piece of work another name for *man*.

1. *The Riverside Shakespeare*

2. *The Signet Shakespeare*

3. *The Arden Shakespeare*

DAILY ROUND

In a rush, he cuts himself while shaving—
three sharp nicks: they sting and pause and bleed.
Irked (his are tailored shirts), he stops each cut
with rips of tissue, dresses, leaves for work.
At a light, he rubs the clotted paper
from his face and shifts the rearview mirror,
curious about the damage to his chin.

Instead the backward backdrop startles him
with something that he's never seen straight on:
Each roadside tree is barbered, the wide boughs
cropped flat so that the aisles of wire
can run between them like a poison vine.
Oak, birch, willow—each is hale and halt:
a sprawl of branches, a sudden making way.

The horn behind him redirects his eye.
He shifts the clutch, tunes the radio,
and finds a song he hasn't heard in years.
The words come back unbidden and he sings,
half wondering how the rootwork marks its loss,
those vanished hemispheres and phantom limbs,
the docked remainder, its odd lopsided bloom.

ON HEARING THAT MUSIC ENHANCES
BRAIN DEVELOPMENT

Listening to music can actually make your child smarter.
  —WTVN REPORT, NOVEMBER 1998

Now that we're *sure* it's good for us,
let's add it to our list of vitamin
supplements and bending exercises
and try to quantify the optimal dose:
volume, duration, daily intervals . . .
We'll need to know, of course, if "jazz"
makes us as smart as "classical"
so that we don't waste any time
on Monk's "Locomotive"
if Bach can turn out better engineers
or Chopin has the keys to dental school.
And just for safety's sake, we'll want
some answers to some lingering concerns:
Does Mingus lead to drug abuse?
Could Tom Waits harm a child?
What about Stravinsky and ADD?

Suppose the surgeon general
had announced the opposite:
that "listening to music" imposes risks
including (but not limited to) heart disease,
emotional disorder, and lapses
into reverie on standard aptitude tests?
Or that every minute you listen
shortens your life by a minute?
I'd almost bet that you could pick

your friends by what they'd keep
and what they'd throw away.
And I'd trade you twenty quiet elevator rides
for a chance to meet the kids
sneaking off to practice
in soundproof basements
and the teachers who'd find them there,
mad-eyed and unhealthy,
in love with something dangerous,
not asking what on earth it does to them.

TYNER

Page Auditorium, Duke University, October 19, 2006

He sat down slowly
and raised his left hand high
above his head
as if he were some barrelhouse
god of sound
raining discord down
on the melody his right hand lifted up.

He spoke perhaps fifty words
all night, his voice salt-weathered
and precise.

"This is in memory of John Coltrane."
"This is a ballad for my former wife."

As he played, his face shook
with the entranced contractions
of uneasy sleep, and when the bright
strobe dissolved his hands
into the keys there was a moment
when his bone-white coat
deranged the light
so that he seemed at once
its terminus and source.

A TRAVELOGUE OF SELF AND SOUL

after Yeats

Try this: Pick a corner of the room,
an upper corner where the three long lines
dead-end in an unmistakable *there*.
Close one eye and aim your finger at this spot
as though your arm's a shotgun and your shot
must split that point in half to save your life.
Be careful. Take all the time you need.
The catch is this: you get no second try.

Satisfied? Keep your hand still. Change eyes.
A sudden lurch means that you've lost the bet—
though we score on the honor system,
and it *is* just a game, a parlor trick,
in which most of us make
a kind of vast and widening unsolved *x*,
a cross of sorts, the depth we take for truth.

TWO

YOUNG GIRL WITH FLUTE

for Lee Sullivan

A man with a wife, three sons, a mortgage,
and a lover is driving to a job
he'd like to quit when he sees a young girl
walking dreamily down the sidewalk,
her head tipped back, singing softly to herself,
innocent, fragile, almost birdlike,
as if she could be startled into flight
or silence. She's carrying a flute case,
swinging it gently as she nears the stop
where the others, oblivious of her,
roughhouse in the street. By coincidence
Rampal is playing on the radio,
though the volume is so low we can't be sure
the man hears it—or if this happenstance
contributes to the upturn in his mood
(as yet not quite perceptible to him)
that seems to come from looking at the girl
in the moment of thought he gives her
until the traffic starts and he moves on.
Soon she's part of the landscape he observes,
or half observes, a couple times a week,
often inadvertently, preoccupied with work
and women—his lies and his mistakes—
and glad for something hopeful to look at
in much the way he'd notice that the trees
were turning green or a hedge were trimmed:
The girl with the flute is taller this year.
Her instrument looks new. Her music books . . .
Had she stopped coming, had she moved away,

or had he found another job and driven
another way to work, the girl might well
have passed unnoticed from his memory.
Instead, one August morning someone new
catches his eye: She's tall, well-shaped,
wearing clothes that hold his gaze a while
despite her age, despite a sense of guilt,
till all at once he sees that it's the girl,
without the flute. Day after day, she brings
a purse, some books, her lunch, but nothing else—
and though he doesn't know the slightest thing
about her gift, her repertoire, her dreams,
he feels, however foolishly, a sense of loss
as though he's watched a branch snap off
some roadside oak and wonders what gave way,
imagining the faint sound of wind
in the dry leaves or the dumbstruck birds
vanished like a melody—Galway? Rampal?—
he might have noticed once but can't recall.

A CURIOSITY

for Miles Davis

My vinyl copy of *In a Silent Way*
is thirty-three years old. I've played it
maybe 10,000 times and still the strange
Galápagos of sound seems freighted
with the grand and awful menace
of our own caged thunder and current,
a pulsing hemisphere of urge and recollection.
Listen. The first tune he named "Shhh."

Last night I noticed the impress of the album
has begun to show through his photo
so that the profiled shock of black
on black, the soft recusant eyes,
grooved brow, and trumpet-split lip
are gathered in a perfect rim of light.

IF MY FRIEND SHOULD TELL ME

for Lindsay Jones

If my friend should tell me
that his wish had been granted,
that for just ten seconds
his blind eyes
could take one perfect image
from the world,
this is what I would do:
lead him by the hand
and stand in front of you.

How could I prepare him?
What words foretell a face
in which he'd find
the sum of all he's missed
since he was born—
the gemmed light of stars
against the sea, hillside autumn,
lilacs after rain, the pure
blue-bordered center of a flame?

AT THE PARK

You said the swans had necks like question marks,
that water's truth was dark and answerless,
and all reflection just the bending back
of light or mind before a flood of stone.

You asked me how I'd live when she was gone
and in the dirt drew this—?—half a heart,
beneath which pooled one resinous drop of blood.

IN THE WALLS

It began as the faintest rustling
under the counter, a glimpse
of next-to-nothing when the light
came on. Everything got still
as soon as we looked or listened,
and so, hoping there was nothing to find,
we went on for a time, finding nothing.

One morning: shit in the fruit bowl,
tooth marks on the apples and pears.
One night, the racket in the wastebasket
grew unignorable. Though we entered
the kitchen noisily, hoping like cowards
to scare them out of sight, they lingered,
emboldened and at home, forcing us to act.

We meant to make a clean end of it.
We hoped to be swift and humane.
We bought harmless plastic boxes
and quick steel traps. When those failed,
we put aside scruples. We wanted it over.
Let them eat their fill of the poison baits.
Let them sicken and die in the walls.

SURGERY ROTATION

You explained that something had been wrong
from the start, a misconception:
one life that briefly looked like two.

Something vital had failed to develop
and died, though the attachment
remained, deforming and unhealthy,
draining life from the viable one,
and needed to be severed—quickly,
decisively. You described four legs,
a collapsed backpack of teeth and hair,
how you could disentangle her
and leave no scar.

We were eating breakfast. Eggs and tea.
For the first time all summer,
you spoke with a kind of glee,
the week you said, "I want to be a surgeon"
and ended things with me.

SLOW DISSOLVE

No umbrella is wide enough
for two people
who no longer care to touch.
The runoff seeps
into their hunched shoulders
and they step
squarely into puddles,
their strides altered
to a pace that suits neither.
Through the slow dissolve
they walk like penitents,
heads bowed in sacrifice,
no one keeping dry.

SEPARATION

At the end he put his books in suitcases.
Then he filled a bag with letters and photographs.
He didn't linger over them. He decided
leave it/keep it. He acted with dispatch.
Next he wrapped plates and glasses in newspaper.
He focused on the headlines as he worked
and packed three boxes from the liquor store:
Dewar's, Jack Daniel's, Johnnie Walker Black.

When that was done he zipped his sleeping bag
around the smaller of their two TVs
and put it in the front seat of his truck.
The shoulder harness fastened it in place.

He went back to get two pictures off the walls—
a framed poster of Ali and Frazier,
and a three-by-four-foot map of the world.
He propped them side by side against the cab.

Then, dazed and short of breath,
he knelt beside the fighters. Their eyes
were fixed with malice, wild with pain.

He looked away and thought about the map—
how quickly it broke down at the extremes,
how hard it was to get those places right:

the wastes of Greenland swollen like a corpse,

the locked Antarctic fractured on a line.

LAUNDRY BAG

Forgetting that he'd thrown it on the bed,
he turns and thinks of her, pours one small drink,
confronts the week of dishes in his sink.
Still out of soap, he lies back down instead.

"*Christ!*" he screams. The bag's as warm as flesh,
a thermal whirl of arms and legs and toes
whose touch provokes a real if brief distress—
no threat, no comfort, just his unlimbed clothes.

ANOTHER AUTUMN

Not like the dying, but like lovers spurned,
leaves grow more gaudy as they starve
in the cold glare of familiar eyes,
begging to be looked at one more time.
"I've changed," they shout, decked out in mustard sleeves
and wrinkled burgundy. Their fruitless pleas
fade to undelicious shades of red.
Without the power to tempt, they writhe and dance
an awkward, doomed, pathetic little jig
to the empty and reflexive noise of wind
and stiffening wood, unable to accept or deny
that something at the core has turned against them.
By late November when the thankful gather,
what's left is bagged like trash along the curb.
No record of that brilliant week or two
inside the widening ring of what endures.

ATALANTA

No swooning temptress, no coy persuasive Eve,
could lance the boar that ravaged Calydon
or skewer a pair of centaurs and outrun
the swift young suitors all hopped up to cleave
enraptured to the bucking of her hips.
Fuck or fight—she'd grind them into dust,
unmoved by pity for their puny lust,
as staunch as any man on Jason's ships.

What tunes this mythos to its opposite?
What trick of meaning coils in the conceit
that paints Arcady's queen with Eden's face,
turns man-tripped huntress toward the snake-eyed wife
and strands them both inside this paraphrase?
An outcast apple made her lose a race.

OUR SENTENCE

Are you saying at-om or Ad-am . . . ?
—JACK KEROUAC TO WILLIAM F. BUCKLEY, *FIRING LINE,* 1968

If the earth and all our knowledge
were to vanish (in fire, say, or ice)
and just one sentence could be passed along
to creatures elsewhere in the universe
by way of summing up what we had learned
of truth eternal to such hearts and minds
as time and place afforded us to own,
those in positions best to know suggest
some form of the atomic postulate.

To wit: We found that earthly bodies
were tormenting things to mind—racing
here and there in heated recklessness,
attracting one another when apart,
but apt to turn repulsive just like that
once they achieved some close proximity.

VILLAINOUS

A contranym's the opposite of itself.
Like poets, battered stepchildren, and whores,
it always holds back something of the truth.

A strong-armed *buckle* weak-kneed in collapse . . .
No need to look for rhyme or reason here.
A contranym's the opposite of itself.

"By indirection find . . ." you're at a loss.
Stand still. Stop trying. Less might soon be more
if you can hold back something of the truth.

"Rage, rage," it raves against the good in death
and claims your broken heart is "no disaster."
A contranym's the opposite of itself.

It shouts, "I hate you," as it pulls you close.
The heart it *cleaves* might fracture or adhere
though neither one of them is quite the truth.

The thing that turned you on? I turned it off.
Figure-ground-figure-ground-figure.
A contranym's the opposite of itself.
It always holds back something. That's the truth.

THREE

McMURDO SOUND

Full grown, a Weddell seal can hold its breath
for more than an hour. It can survive
ten weeks without food, water, sunlight,
or others of its kind. Owl-eyed, tuberous,
it can dive 1,500 feet beneath the roof
of the Antarctic, then chew through a floe
to the open air. The gelid verge
sustains it, far from shore. And it thrives.

A month in captivity and it dies.
Invariant cold, the careful habitat,
live fish and krill are wasted effort:
It breaks its teeth against the walls
it thinks are freezing inward. Fever kills it,
whose earth, 'til then, was water, ice, and sky.

AN URBAN MYTH

On vacation, a woman finds a dog,
no tags, unwashed, mangy, a mutt,
funny-looking too, his tail broken,
his shoulders rounded,
his eyes quick and close together
under oily fur.

Timid at first, he eats from a dish,
starts to hang around,
licks her hand.

Back home she keeps him indoors,
but he's slow to learn,
doesn't fetch or speak or walk on a leash—
though when she shakes the box of food,
he comes,
awkward,
low to the ground.

One night, home late from work,
she finds the cat in pieces,
the dog asleep on the linoleum,
blood on his muzzle.

The vet's grimace quickens his voice:
"That thing is no pet.
In Brazil they're *luparatas*—wolf rats.
They come in ships, live on dockyards.
Scavengers,
they eat fish heads and garbage."

It's put to sleep and burned.
Years pass.
No change quite rids her of it. No friend.
At each new place,
she thinks of how it moved against her night—
unjungled, restless, angling through the dark.
Thinks too how easily she was fooled:
choosing a name, taking its need for her own,
misunderstanding.

AT THE WOLF CAGE, SENECA PARK, 1980

for Darrin and Danny McBride

Years later I learned that howling
helped them gather the pack,
that they ordered their distances this way:
a note through the dark barrens
for those who had lost the trail.

That day, we thought the cage was empty
until a siren set them off:
eyes closed, heads back,
they came within five feet of us,
crowding together, raising the alarm.

In school I said a prayer
whenever I heard that sound:
". . . now and at the hour of our death . . ."
The cadence moved me: killers, lost things.
I felt it in the hair along my spine.

All winter now I feel it.
Twice a night, more, this city stirs.
"What do they want?" you asked me,
half my age, frightened by the noise.
My lie meant this: *I hope we don't find out.*

URSA MINOR

Language is like a cracked kettle on which we beat out tunes to make
bears dance while all the time we long to move the stars to pity.
                    —GUSTAVE FLAUBERT

What's pitiful is whining at the stars
for being globes of fire instead of eyes
all gazing down at you in sympathy
like some fat, doting nanny from Rouen
indifferent to the suffering in the street
(the crippled boy, the heartsick suicide)
unless it's been ennobled by your pen
and lifted into deadly, deathless prose.

Gustave, I hear the stars are reading lamps,
beneath each one—a billion Francophiles.
I shipped your novels at the speed of light.
The tears should start in 20 million years.
Come on . . . let's celebrate . . . go see the bears.
I want to hear the words that make them dance.

THE BIRD FEEDER

The day I set it up and bought the seed,
I only hoped to kill an afternoon,
clean out a closet, and address the need
my nephews' gifts create: not to impugn
their clumsy, heartfelt caring. About birds,
I didn't really know a goddamned thing,
and so I grudged an hour to learn the words
my chart called "crucial rudiments." (A wing,
for instance, is topped by *coverts,* trailed by
rectricies.) Duty at first . . . then . . . something more,
all unexpectedly, a sense that I
might find some larger purpose in this chore
(like Saint Francis or the guy at Alcatraz).
Man's bond with nature . . . wildlife . . . all of that.

Or so it seemed each night when I'd return
to find the pegs packed tight with feathered throngs,
whose calls and genders I could soon discern.
Sort of. The slow, bookish work absorbing songs
and shapes and colors proved a solemn joy
as did my sundry schemes to lure them in:
suet baskets, extra thistle seed, decoy
drops for squirrels and grackles (their vulturine
raids drive off "the finer breeds"), rags (for nests),
water, peanut butter scrubbed on corky bark . . .
That done, my hopes expanded—would my guests,
kaleidoscopic, tamed, and prodigal,
cross continents to daze their patriarch?
My eyes were wide for everything and all.

But mainly I got sparrows, finches, doves.
Common stuff. I still watch them with my meals
though less devoutly now: one of love's
habituations and all that can conceal
of guilt and peevishness, the gray routine
mornings (up at five, my coffee on the lawn)
expecting . . . what? Parrots? Owls? I'd not foreseen
how meager were the bounds my heart had drawn,
how day by day I'd find a way to lose
my feeling for the ones who needed me.
And though they'll take what's given carelessly—
not caring—that's a clumsy business too.
It lights like blackbirds falling with the snow,
a hungry darkness, sprawling to and fro.

FATHER DAMIEN OF MOLOKAI

A century ago Hawaiian blood froze at the very name "Molokai."
Lepers waded through this surf to await death.
                    —FROM THE DAMIEN MUSEUM, HONOLULU

As a boy, I heard *"leopard* colony"
and dreamed of joining him for a glimpse
of the big cats with the terrifying skin.
At night, in bed, I'd whisper
"Da-mi-en of Mol-o-kai . . ."
each syllable mysterious and transporting,
like "Jesus of Nazareth" or "Tarzan of the Apes."
Stark photographs revealed
the cats' appalling appetite for flesh,
the wounds that never healed,
the wasted, dying, brown-eyed
natives Damien had come to save.
He helped them by the thousands
through their final hours,
knowing his own would come,
a gorgeous head tearing cassock and collar,
limb from noble, careworn limb.

Sahib! Where the leopard walks,
he brushes out his tracks with his tail!

My teacher brushed away a smile
at the symmetry of my mistake:
"Like Daniel in the Lion's Den?" she asked.
I thought of that, years later,
walking on the sand at Waikiki
the week they closed the Father Damien Museum,

54

which I'd stumbled on by accident,
while shopping for sunscreen, my white legs
slippery with coconut oil,
my mind on sunburn and melanoma—
an unheroic, uncontagious man.
By then, I knew that both *Bacillus leprae*
and *Panthera pardus* had survived the flood,
that Hawaii had no cats worth speaking of,
that god's work was stranger than it seemed.
I'd learned, as well, that most of us forgo
the swift drama of the muscled beast—
that there are other ways to be destroyed.
I knew that you could walk
for years along the shores of Molokai
and not see what was eating you alive.

HORSEMAN, PASS BY: A LUNAR ECLIPSE

Cast a cold eye / on life, on death
—W. B. YEATS

We could see it perfectly from the grandstand
at Batavia Downs. By the second race,
the moon had risen above the tote board,
and by the fourth, our shadow
was nosing into view across the moon.
It was a night for long shots—trifectas in particular
according to the PA announcer,
whose eye for correspondences
was tuned to our own. At every lull,
he'd shift from the sulkies to the sky:
"Above the backstretch now, it's Earth's Umbra
moving three-wide through the turn,
Lunar Lady fading,
SunRaycer blocked out along the rail."
It didn't take an astronomer
to sense the gravity of the event,
how it showed us in a special light,
the horses and the horse-drawn wheels
tilting and whirling around a track
that was itself in orbit. The wide sky
kept us in our seats. So did the numbered colts.
Though we never found a connection
between the two lineups (Dark Satellite
finished fifth; Ecliptic pulled up lame)
we wouldn't quite dismiss it all the same.
Between the laws of motion and emotion,
we drank to both—Miller Draft
in plastic cups—and watched the moon's pilsner

run to wine. All night we tipped
the field glasses back and forth, trying
to strike a balance, and hedging
a bit—an eye on the heavens,
an eye on our two-dollar bets.

CAVE CANEM

Say what you want about the begging,
the shit in the yard, the fleas.
I agree. Both drool and digging
make a mess, and I've vacuumed
hair enough to stuff a couch.
More than once, our nightly walk
has filled me with contempt for his wordless
mind, his need to sniff and piss.

But I have seen him rise
sick from a sound sleep
to stand in readiness at the door,
and I have measured the dark
in his growl: wind, friend,
stranger—you are not his match.

MAN IN THE MOON

Back on earth, a pot of crater ash
behaves like topsoil. Apples grow in it.
So do rice and roses—cacti, ginseng, limes.
The greenhouses at NASA fairly burst
with shelves marked *Sea of Crises, Lake of Death.*
Each quick transition (pit into pith)
seemed oddly reckoned by the foreign cores,
their tilt and texture perfect,
their drainage like a fine Nebraska loam.
One botanist grew tulips that he swore
were bordered in a shade he'd never seen.
"Green cheese," his student called it.
He kept them in a cooler with the grapes
they crushed to make a jar of lunar wine.

Who isn't heartened at this news?
Walking the dog, watching night come on,
who hasn't wished to feel that livening change—
the long blight broken, the spell undone,
the savior braving darkness and long odds
to bring us, finally, all the joy we're owed?
Who doesn't weary of our own strange orbit,
brooding about the rank and fertile earth,
unable to face it, unable to turn away?

At school, Darwin's last book was my favorite.
It pleased me to think of the old scholar
pounding the piano at his pots of worms
("Completely deaf," he found) or setting out
turnips and horseradish, strips of raw meat
("Night after night they could be seen tugging
at them . . . the edges of the pieces engulfed
in their mouths"). Part of it was sheer charm—
the great man with a ball of cotton wool
between his teeth, blowing millefleurs perfume
across the worm sward. But it was more than that.
Kneeling in the mud at Kent and Surrey,
weighing the castings, trying to puzzle out
the vague calligraphies of fingered earth,
he showed me how the world was undermined
by these small turnings, that the Roman town
at Shropshire and the flagstones in my yard
had foundered in the same loosening warp,
two inches deeper every dozen years.
Here was a pace that I had not conceived,
the slow dirt-eaters' unremitting ounce
summed endlessly, a whole landscape leveled
by the windblown cleats. I felt the dull ground
take shape around me. I would learn to watch.

One day last spring, I started to reread
the old volume. I've got a shaded porch
where I can sit and think or fall asleep
as the mood takes me, but that afternoon
the sky was lit with what the weathermen
call *virga*—high sun-bound scatterings of rain
that drift like crystals through the drying air

and disappear in flight. For an hour,
a tantalus of gold and violet
descended on me, each brief drop
consumed in a fiery spark of ice.
Only once did I turn away to look down
at the book. More than Darwin's words
or figures, what struck me at that instant
were the notes I'd written in the margins—
not the substance of them, but the script itself,
the careful rungs and curvatures of a hand
no longer mine. Here was a change
that I had not conceived, a faint constriction,
blunt and coarsening. *"The work
of worms"* stood out against the page.
I had no heart for it. Far overhead,
the quick regenerate mist had been dispelled.
I put the book aside and shut my eyes.

TO A FRIEND WHOSE WORK HAS COME TO NOTHING

after Yeats

Consider the blue-footed booby, the impressionistic
elegance of his guano pleasure dome,
the subtle pastels applied *alla prima*—
"at one sitting"—from his seafood palette:
anchovies and sardines fine-tuned in his excreta.
Study the webbed brushwork—bold, masterful—
his pharaoh-like economy of form:
nests without straw; nests without the merest tree
. from which to gather, in his driftwood bill,
the staples of his rearguard phylum-mates.
Watch him attack his detractors: gulls
crosshairing his young, land crabs, rats,
one's own too-close-for-comfort toe.
Find the line, midway through the ring,
at which he springs to action: his thrusted head
a stiletto; his broad, pale scapulars
hooding his intent. Only what's inside
that perimeter merits his concern. Consider this:
His own chicks, expelled through feeding rivalries,
turn unrecognizable. He lets them starve
or clubs them lifeless with his turquoise feet,
one plump descendent preferable to a clutch
of half-fed risky business. Insular,
spartan, self-contained—his life subsumes such loss.
There's absolution in his tapered skull,
the trip-switch of his birdbrained synapses,
the clear, precoded message telling him
to shit in a circle. To care for that.

BY BLUE ONTARIO'S SHORE

for Mark McBride

We skipped school and went down to the lake.
While Sister Myra bored our history class,
we stopped a French-Canadian attack
with driftwood rifles. In place of math,
we raced across infinities of sand.
Science was our buoyant boyish flesh,
the curved horizon, and the names of fish.
In English, we were Long John Silver's band.

At noon we met the ancient mariner
and asked him what was biting. "A week's meals,"
he sneered, tapping a bucket with his rod.
The surface roiled—black and thick with eels.
We ran. Remember? The thrill of it? The fear?
The first time you said, "There isn't any god"?

He had a hand-tied rosary as a kid;
it hung around his bedpost like a noose
made out of knots he couldn't slip: They preyed
on him until he prayed on them. God knows . . .
faith doesn't count, but one night the boy did
and saw that from the first he'd been misled:
a Hail Mary missing! Caught in the breach,
he felt as if he'd peeked beneath her dress
and found her wanting—a crack in the stained
glass of his devotion, a doubting Thomas
with his doubts confirmed. Shaken, unrestrained,
for days he tried to pray the prayers he'd missed,
held on to nothing where the string was flawed,
and filled the empty space with words to god.

DON'T USE MY BLOOD

The Confidential Self-Exclusion Sticker lets the donor indicate
anonymously that his/her blood should not be used for transfusion
if he/she is donating under peer pressure or other strained
circumstances.

—THE AMERICAN RED CROSS

Don't trust my smile
no matter how I gush
at you from the tilted chair
letting blood
run into your plastic bag.
My heart is sick. My pint is venomous.

Don't trust my words.
I lied to every question on your form.
I have "taken/given money in exchange for sex"
with men and women,
not "even once," but many times.
I've been "unprotected" in love,
in despair, in loneliness—
in New York and Miami,
in Java and in Niamey, Niger.
I lived through those connections.
That's why I come to you.

Don't trust my eyes.
Though I look away from the quick stab
into the swabbed and swollen mainline
of my tied-off radial vein,
I'm not afraid. I share ungodly needles
all the time. Like yours

they make me feel giddy and generous,
light-headed and brave.
Unpunctured night
turns rank and malarial.
Rats have bitten me.
Such things leave their mark.

Don't use my blood.
I offer it for nothing,
a sacrament unfit for you to touch.
Tape your red cross
in the hinge of my arm.
Take the scarlet button,
pin it to my chest.
Change *Be nice,*
I gave blood today.
Write *Love me,*
I have drained my heart.

THE WORLD'S FARE

Stuck in traffic, harnessed to his seat,
Flynn drifts away from *All Things Considered*
and considers (of all things) the backsides
of women hurrying to cross the street.

So it has gone: the Great Books on Tape,
the French Made Easy, the boxed cassettes
on Happiness at Home—all his attempts
at self-improvement on the way to work

sideswiped by a girl in running shorts,
a billboard jingle or a neon light—
the smell of onions, meat, and sweetened grease.
Just now a slight wind shifts a flowered skirt . . .

"Thirty years ago this week, the New York
World's Fair opened what organizers called
the 'Olympics of Progress' on the reclaimed
swamplands outside of Flushing Meadow.

More than fifty nations set up pavilions
that previewed an ordered urban landscape
where science, gadgetry, and automated roads
promised us time to cultivate our dreams . . ."

Three horn blasts and a loud "Let's go *FUCK*head,"
recall Flynn to the gap in traffic
and to NPR. He lifts one finger
in a cold salute. Noses forward. Waits.

"At the Ford Exhibit, visitors took
new convertibles on a twelve-minute
half-mile ride from the dawn of history
to the shining 'City of Tomorrow' . . .

At the Hall of Science, UpJohn built
an inflated human brain twenty-four feet
in diameter. Flashbulbs sped along tubes
to show the way we process what we see."

Flynn feels a sullen disconnection.
How little flashes back or speeds along . . .
He'd had a cherry snow cone near a globe
of some sort . . . though they'd used another word . . .

"An iron 'Unisphere' twelve stories tall
served as the heart and emblem of the Fair,
whose motto, 'Peace Through Understanding,'
was depicted by a team from U.S. Steel."

Flynn tilts his visor to the shifting glare
and glances in his rearview mirror,
returning now to the one ride at the Fair
he's never forgotten. On the last day

he walked off from the group and made his way
to the gates of I-N-D-I-A. For fifty cents
they led him up a wooden platform
and put him on a blanket draped across

the spine of a sedated elephant.
It tramped a circle through a trampled field.
What Flynn liked best about the Fair,
was running his hand along that muddy back.

POWERS

Nights, Flynn studies remedial math
at the local high school. *"Empowerment
through knowledge!"* the teacher chants.
He tells them it's a self-defeating myth,
all the crap they've heard that some people just can't
work with numbers. "If you're *enumerate*,"
he says, "if you're not equipped to cope with
fundamental notions of number and chance,
then the system has cheated you." Flynn nods.
(A *megaton*? A *kilobyte*? A *trillion*-dollar debt?)
He learns that he can't hope to beat the odds
they've stacked against him—not till his "blind faith
in sanitized truth and ad-man facts"
gives place to "the power of his own mind."
This course will help him. One step at a time.

The key, he's told, is to grasp the principles
and build on what he already knows.
Thus primed, Flynn confronts the higher powers:
>   *If 10^3 is 10 three times itself—or 1,000,*
>   *and 10^2 is 10 two times itself—or 100,*
>   *and 10^1 is 10 one times itself—or 10,*
>   *then 10^0 must be 10 zero times itself—or 0.*
"Well . . . umm . . . *no*," the teacher says. "It equals one,
although the reasoning is . . . somewhat involved
and the class, perhaps, should just . . . accept the fact . . ."
A small concession, but in it Flynn recalls
his first attempt at this long years before—
the clouding of his mind before the proofs,
the moving on before things quite add up.

Already he feels his old negatives starting to multiply,
which he's been told become positives somehow
though he'd be damned if he could tell you why.

SELF-ASSESSMENT IN A HOTEL MEN'S ROOM

The test of a first-rate intelligence is the ability to hold two opposing
ideas in mind at the same time and still retain the ability to function.
—F. SCOTT FITZGERALD

Pensive at the urinal,
Flynn thinks, "I need another drink"
and (simultaneous with this)
"I need to stop. I've drunk too much."

Absorbed in these antitheses,
he nonetheless (with grace) emits
a straight sure-handed stream of piss
precisely where he's aiming it.

Indecisive but still continent, he conjures Fitz:
the prose and cons. Washing up, he winks
at his reflection. "First-rate," he thinks,
"and full of shit." Like the drink
he wants to order. And decline.
Don't ask him what makes up his mind.

ZALE

The most two-sided fights ever.
—RED SMITH ON THE ZALE-GRAZIANO TRILOGY

He forged himself from scraps in Gary's mills:
Zaleski—tempered—pounded down to Zale.
A talent for attrition vs. the skills
of lesser-mettled foes. The "Man of Steel"
gave and took: quick fists, concussive power,
dead game, but easy to hit, dazed or downed
by journeymen, stopped twice in '34,
lost 16 times before he won the crown.

A kid, I'd lost fights too. Tunney, Monzón,
Robinson, Ali . . . were graceful, perfect.
Not like me. But Zale! The last heroic
fantasy to fall: staggered, outmanned,
spent, bloodied, and almost at the end,
he flattened Graziano with a broken hand.

72

THE AFGHAN BUDDHAS

for Michele Jozwiak

Their eyes were closed, not like the eyes of men
dragged out in blindfolds to the firing squad,
but calm and inward-looking: unattached.
All things arise, they know, and all things pass.

Their eyes are open, who can't bear to see
the graven idols of another faith,
who fear what moves them and whose laws forsake
the draped affliction of a woman's face.

Twin towers in the cliffs of Bamiyan
stood 1,300 years. Now they are gone,
not like Ozymandias, king of kings,
not year-by-year succumbing to the sand,
but in an instant shattered—the stark end
accelerating like the jets unloosed
by antique travelers in the modern land.

—I.M. 09.11.01

THE WHITE DOVES OF MAZAR

for Nabilia

For crusts of bread
these sacred birds entrust
their bodies to your hands
despite the evidence of blood
in every street
and twenty-seven years of war.
Though nothing will change
for the Hazaras and Uzbeks,
the Pashtuns and Tajiks,
the Arabs, Russians, and Americans
try nonetheless to feel
the slight heartbeat
against your palms. Touch
the ruffed head
and trembling wings—
helpless now and beautiful—
as if they were the framed,
unfinished faces of the dead.

AMONTILLADO

"You can tear them down for all I care,"
says the old woman, rapping a knuckle
on the slipshod walls her late husband
put up years ago to subdivide
the open spaces of the house
she needs to sell—though not bad enough
to have washed the sinks or to smile
when she adds, in a tone worn thin
as her housecoat, "He was a shitty carpenter . . .
among other things." She has a manner
made for walls, so I stick to the facts
about plumbing and wiring, septic tanks,
and the condition of the roof.
My wife of two months says the place
has character. The large front porch
and high ceilings remind her of the house
she lived in as a girl. "There's life in it,"
she says. "And with some fixing up . . ."

Six weeks later, I'm standing
where the dead man stood, hammer
and bar undoing what I've no skill
to set right. Crushed plaster dusts the floor
like a crime scene. I brace myself for skeletons.
Instead, concealed in gaps and pigeonholes,
as if to mark his stopping point each night,
are 24 empty pints of Traveler's Club vodka.
I string them in a line along a ledge
the frost has heaved for years all out of true
like things she might have said to comfort him
or thoughts in drink of how he'd sober up
and either make it right or walk away:

"I'm going out to get some cigarettes . . ."
Though the wood is splintered and the nail heads bend
against themselves ("Irish trim," his wife called it),
he screwed the cap on each dead soldier,
the price tag folded once and dropped inside
like the razor blades he dropped behind the sink:
Hennessey's Fine Liquors: $2.98 + tax.
The words have bled and hardened in the neck,
notes from an island, at the bottom of the sea.

CHARACTER AS FATE: THE LIMITS OF FORMULAE

Character is fate.
>   —HERACLITUS

Oedipus determines his own conduct, by being the man he is . . .
This correspondence between his character and his fate removes
the obstacle to our full acceptance of the play.
>   —*THE NORTON ANTHOLOGY OF WORLD MASTERPIECES*

Not quite the philosophy of just desserts,
it nonetheless suggests that a reckless wit
placed behind a team of cautious nags
will find a way to steer them off the road
and show up later strangled in the reins.
His opposite—the sober, modest type—
though given just a bareback of a chance,
nine times in ten will find his way to town.
He saves the day. He weds the heroine.

This helps some students out in freshman lit,
provided none of them has owned a horse:
Put Oedipus, his hubris and brains,
atop a bitless mount that wants him off,
you'll get one mother-fucker of a ride
and afterward sit divvying the blame
in careful piles you've logically foreseen—
the lie of which is that you'll ever know
what's going on inside a horse's head.

It gets them through a paper, past a test.
The rest they'll learn—or not—outside of class,

where some of them perhaps will chance to think
how horse and horseman always form a third,
beyond all explanation, undivined.
"It seems to me," I had a student say,
"what crashes crashes, and what doesn't don't,"
which left us more or less where we began:
with god and chemistry and metaphor and man.

green press
INITIATIVE

Northwestern University Press is committed to preserving ancient forests and natural resources. We elected to print this title on 30% post consumer recycled paper, processed chlorine free. As a result, for this printing, we have saved:

2 Trees (40' tall and 6-8" diameter)
841 Gallons of Wastewater
1 Million BTUs of Total Energy
51 Pounds of Solid Waste
175 Pounds of Greenhouse Gases

Northwestern University Press made this paper choice because our printer, Thomson-Shore, Inc., is a member of Green Press Initiative, a nonprofit program dedicated to supporting authors, publishers, and suppliers in their efforts to reduce their use of fiber obtained from endangered forests.

For more information, visit www.greenpressinitiative.org

Environmental impact estimates were made using the Environmental Defense Paper Calculator. For more information visit: www.papercalculator.org.